POSTWAR AMERICA

THE WOMEN'S RIGHTS MOVEMENT

by Gertrude R. Becker

T0020291

FOCUS
READERS.

NAVIGATOR

WWW.FOCUSREADERS.COM

Copyright © 2024 by Focus Readers®, Mendota Heights, MN 55120. All rights reserved. No part of this book may be reproduced or utilized in any form or by any means without written permission from the publisher.

Focus Readers is distributed by North Star Editions:
sales@northstareditions.com | 888-417-0195

Produced for Focus Readers by Red Line Editorial.

Content Consultant: Louise Newman, PhD, Associate Professor of History, University of Florida

Photographs ©: Dennis Cook/AP Images, cover, 1; Shutterstock Images, 4–5, 27; Howard Liberman/Library of Congress, 7; AP Images, 9, 10–11, 13, 17, 21, 23; Michael Maloney/San Francisco Chronicle/AP Images, 14; Joe Marquette/AP Images, 18–19; Saquan Stimpson/ZUMA Press Wire/Cal Sport Media/AP Images, 24–25; Red Line Editorial, 29

Library of Congress Cataloging-in-Publication Data
Names: Becker, Gertrude R., author.
Title: The women's rights movement / by Gertrude R. Becker.
Description: Mendota Heights, MN : Focus Readers, [2024] | Series: Postwar America | Includes bibliographical references and index. | Audience: Grades 4-6
Identifiers: LCCN 2023036582 (print) | LCCN 2023036583 (ebook) | ISBN 9798889980469 (hardcover) | ISBN 9798889980896 (paperback) | ISBN 9798889981701 (pdf) | ISBN 9798889981329 (ebook)
Subjects: LCSH: Women's rights--United States--History--Juvenile literature. | Feminism--United States--History--Juvenile literature.
Classification: LCC HQ1236.5.U6 B43 2024 (print) | LCC HQ1236.5.U6 (ebook) | DDC 305.420973--dc23/eng/20230830
LC record available at https://lccn.loc.gov/2023036582
LC ebook record available at https://lccn.loc.gov/2023036583

Printed in the United States of America
Mankato, MN
012024

ABOUT THE AUTHOR

Gertrude R. Becker lives in Minneapolis, Minnesota. She likes exploring new places and loves anything involving books.

TABLE OF CONTENTS

CHAPTER 1

EARLY EFFORTS

The modern women's rights movement took place in the 1960s and 1970s. However, the struggle for equal rights began much earlier. When the United States was founded, women did not have the same rights as men. They could not vote. They could not run for office. Married women couldn't own property,

Many activists in the 1800s and early 1900s called for women's right to vote. They organized meetings, marches, and protests.

either. **Activists** throughout the 1800s worked to change these inequalities. They often focused on the right to vote. Their actions were part of a movement. It was the first wave of **feminism** in the United States.

VOTING RIGHTS

Women spent decades working to gain voting rights. They used several methods to call for change. They protested and marched. They also wrote speeches and essays. They tried to convince US leaders to make changes. In 1919, Congress passed the Nineteenth **Amendment**. It took effect the next year. It gave women the right to vote. However, other laws still kept most people of color from voting.

During World War II, many women got jobs operating machines in factories.

Other changes took place during World War II (1939–1945). Many men became soldiers. They went overseas to fight. That meant their jobs were left open. US factories needed workers to make weapons and supplies. So, women took over those jobs. More than six million women began working in factories.

After the war, men returned to their jobs. Many women were forced to quit. Strict ideas about gender roles were one reason. People often expected women to stay home and raise kids. Some women continued working. But they were often paid much less than men. Some female workers were also **harassed**. Some were accused of taking away men's jobs.

Many women did not accept these forms of sexism. They wanted to be treated and paid equally. They wanted equal rights outside of workplaces,

Some women formed unions. These groups help workers call for fair pay and fair working conditions.

too. Eventually, these ideas grew into a movement. Activists spoke out and protested. Their work became the women's rights movement of the 1960s and 1970s. The second wave of feminism had begun.

CHAPTER 2

PROGRESS IN THE 1960S

In 1961, the US government formed a **commission**. It studied how schools, workplaces, and laws treated women unfairly. It found that many women were paid less than men for the same jobs. In response, lawmakers passed the Equal Pay Act of 1963. The next year, Congress created the Equal Employment

Aileen Clarke Hernandez was an activist from New York. She was the only woman on the Equal Employment Opportunity Commission.

Opportunity Commission. It aimed to lessen unfair hiring based on gender.

Meanwhile, feminist writers described problems that women faced. For example, Betty Friedan wrote about how women were pressured to be wives and mothers. Other goals, such as having jobs, were looked down on. Friedan said this made many women feel trapped and unhappy. Many readers agreed with her.

In 1966, a group of women formed the National Organization for Women (NOW). NOW wanted new laws to protect women from violence and inequality. More **radical** groups formed, too. They wanted to transform how society saw and treated

In 1963, Betty Friedan published a book called *The Feminine Mystique*. It became a bestseller.

women so women could have more power. This idea was called women's liberation.

All these groups took action. They held sit-ins about workplace unfairness. They marched to protest gender roles. They wrote to lawmakers to change **reproductive** laws.

Dolores Huerta cofounded a union that helped farmworkers.

Activists pushed for changes to divorce laws as well. They wanted women to have more freedom. Some states made new laws that let women start divorces on their own. Before, many needed their husbands' approval. The change helped some women escape harmful marriages.

Meanwhile, leaders such as Dolores Huerta focused on farmworkers' rights. They planned events and marches to help workers. At the same time, they worked to fight sexism.

SHARED GOALS

The women's rights movement shared several goals with the **civil rights movement**. Both movements called for equal treatment. Leaders such as Dorothy Height and Fannie Lou Hamer played key parts in both. Some laws also addressed issues for both movements. The Civil Rights Act of 1964 was one example. It banned job discrimination based on race, religion, and gender.

BLACK FEMINISM

Black women were key leaders in the women's rights movement. They faced racism as well as sexism. White feminists tended not to address racism. But Black feminists described how the two problems were connected.

Pauli Murray was one person who did this. Murray cofounded NOW. Murray described how racism and sexism formed a "dual burden" for Black women.[1] Both problems combined to make their lives harder. So, Murray believed both problems needed to be addressed at once.

The Combahee River Collective (CRC) took that idea even further. This group of Black female leaders formed in 1974. The CRC identified several problems people faced. Those included racism, sexism, and poverty. The CRC believed these problems could not be separated. "We are

Pauli Murray was a lawyer and writer. Murray's work often focused on the problems caused by segregation.

not just trying to fight oppression on one front or even two," they wrote.[2] Instead, they aimed to undo many types of inequality.

The ideas of these writers were early forms of intersectionality. They showed how one person can be part of many different groups. All those groups shape the person's experience. This idea became central to later waves of feminism.

1. Pauli Murray. "The Negro Woman in the Quest for Equality." Speech at the National Council of Negro Women Convention, Washington, DC, 14 Nov. 1963.
2. "The Combahee River Collective Statement." *How We Get Free: Black Feminism and the Combahee River Collective*. Edited by Keeanga-Yamahtta Taylor. Chicago: Haymarket Books, 2017. Print. Page 22.

CHAPTER 3

INTO THE 1970s

Even more changes took place in the 1970s. Several focused on women's safety. Some activists opened women's shelters. Women who were unsafe at home could stay there instead. Activists also set up crisis hotlines. Women could call these phone numbers to get help if strangers or partners hurt them.

Representative Patsy Mink (center) helped write several laws related to women's rights and education.

Some changes helped limit sexism in schools. Patsy Mink helped Congress pass Title IX in 1972. This law made rules for schools that received government money. They had to offer the same options to all students, regardless of gender. As a result, women gained better access to higher education. Their options for sports also improved.

Other changes were related to reproductive rights. In 1972, access to birth control pills widened. Single women could legally use them. In 1973, the Supreme Court ruled on *Roe v. Wade*. This case was about **abortion**. Many states had laws banning abortions. The Supreme

Some people celebrated the *Roe v. Wade* decision. Others gathered to protest it.

Court said those laws were wrong. They went against women's right to privacy. The court made most abortions legal. All these changes gave women more freedom in family planning.

Some activists felt these changes were not enough. They pushed for the Equal Rights Amendment (ERA). It would add protections for women to the Constitution. Creating an amendment is a long process. First, Congress votes on it. Then, three-fourths of states must support it. Congress passed the ERA in 1972. But not enough states supported it. So, the amendment failed.

ABORTION

Roe v. Wade didn't end debates about abortion. Many people disagreed with the ruling. They wanted to limit or ban abortions. Meanwhile, many others supported the ruling. They wanted to keep abortion legal. In 2022, the Supreme Court overturned *Roe v. Wade*. It ruled that states could ban abortion. And many states did.

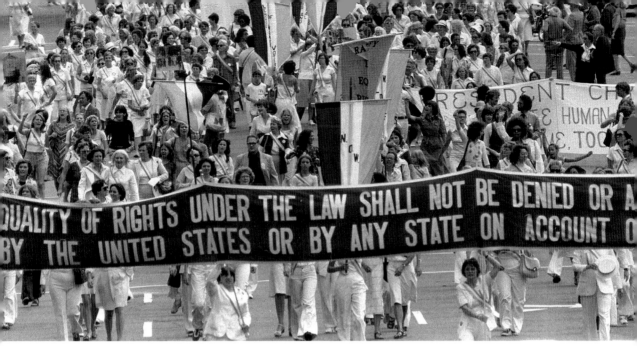

Thousands of people march in support of the Equal
Rights Amendment in 1977.

Meanwhile, the movement faced
conflicts. Many activists disagreed
about how much to push the ERA. The
movement had outside opponents, too.
Some rallied to fight the ERA. Others
opposed abortion rights. Throughout the
1970s, those opponents got stronger. The
movement's strength faded.

CHAPTER 4

THE MOVEMENT'S LEGACY

The women's rights movement has had many lasting impacts. Title IX is one example. The law's main goal was helping women attend college. But it also helped many more women and girls play sports. Laws about divorce and equal pay gave women more options, too. More could support their families or live on their own.

Title IX helped female athletes gain access to more funding and scholarships.

The movement also paved the way for later waves of feminism. In the 1990s, for example, individuality was a key concept. Many women rejected old rules about how to dress or act. They wanted more freedom to express themselves. This included their sexuality. These ideas became part of the third wave of feminism.

Sexual harassment was another important topic. In 1991, Anita Hill spoke in front of the Supreme Court. She said **nominee** Clarence Thomas had sexually harassed her. Thomas joined the court despite this. But Hill's speech was a historic moment.

Millions of women took part in the 2018 Women's March. Sexual harassment was one of the problems they wanted to call out.

In the 2010s, social media helped a fourth wave of feminism begin. The focus on sexual harassment continued. The #MeToo movement was a key part of that focus.

The women's rights movement also inspired other activists. The LGBTQ+ movement is one example. Its leaders often used court cases to fight for rights. Many drew examples from the women's rights movement.

The women's rights movement brought many changes. But activists are still working to help all genders be treated equally. Some work to put more women

LEADERSHIP GAP

In 2018, women made up 50.8 percent of the US population. They held approximately half of all jobs. But in many fields, women had less than half of leadership roles. In 2023, for example, only 12 of 50 state governors were women. This difference is called the women's leadership gap. The gap has decreased over time. But it still exists.

in leadership roles. Some fight to expand reproductive rights. Others help make equal pay more certain. Like activists before them, they continue calling for change.

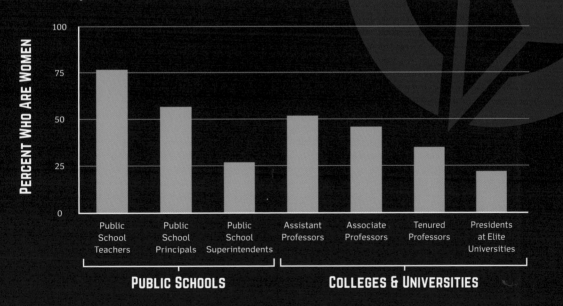

LEADERSHIP GAP IN EDUCATION

In the 2020s, women were less likely to hold high-level positions in education-related jobs.

PERCENT WHO ARE WOMEN

100

75

50

25

0

| Public School Teachers | Public School Principals | Public School Superintendents | Assistant Professors | Associate Professors | Tenured Professors | Presidents at Elite Universities |

PUBLIC SCHOOLS   COLLEGES & UNIVERSITIES

FOCUS ON
THE WOMEN'S RIGHTS MOVEMENT

Write your answers on a separate piece of paper.

1. Write a few sentences explaining the main ideas of Chapter 1.

2. Do you think changing laws or changing people's opinions is more important for improving equality? Why?

3. In what year did Title IX become law?
   - **A.** 1961
   - **B.** 1966
   - **C.** 1972

4. Why might activists want more women in leadership roles?
   - **A.** Women are faster at making decisions than men are.
   - **B.** Women could then make decisions that help other women.
   - **C.** Women could use those leadership roles to ignore laws.

Answer key on page 32.

GLOSSARY

abortion
A medical end to a pregnancy.

activists
People who take action to make social or political changes.

amendment
A change or addition to the US Constitution.

civil rights movement
A mass struggle against racial discrimination in the United States in the 1950s and 1960s.

commission
A group formed to do a specific job for the government.

feminism
The belief in equal rights for women and men.

harassed
Hurt, insulted, or made to feel unsafe or uncomfortable.

nominee
A person who is being suggested for a job.

radical
Having extreme ideas about a topic.

reproductive
Related to having children.

TO LEARN MORE

BOOKS

Felix, Rebecca. *#WomensMarch: Insisting on Equality.* Minneapolis: Abdo Publishing, 2020.

Harris, Duchess, with Deirdre R. J. Head. *Barbara Jordan: Politician and Civil Rights Leader.* Minneapolis: Abdo Publishing, 2019.

Harris, Duchess, with Marne Ventura. *Fannie Lou Hamer: Civil Rights Activist.* Minneapolis: Abdo Publishing: 2020.

NOTE TO EDUCATORS

Visit **www.focusreaders.com** to find lesson plans, activities, links, and other resources related to this title.

INDEX

Answer Key: 1. Answers will vary; 2. Answers will vary; 3. C; 4. B